There Goes
The Neighbourhood

An Irreverent History of Canada

There Goes
The Neighbourhood

An Irreverent History of Canada

Adrian Raeside

DOUBLEDAY CANADA LIMITED

Canadian Cataloguing in Publication Data

Raeside, Adrian, 1957 –
    There goes the neighbourhood : an irreverent history of Canada.

ISBN 0–385–25392–3

1. Canada – History – Caricatures and cartoons.   2. Canadian wit and humor,
Pictorial. 3. Canada – History – Humor. I. Title.

NC1449.R34A4 1992 971'.00207 C92–094631–3

Design by Tania Craan

Printed on acid-free paper
Typeset by MacTrix DTP
Printed and bound in Canada by Best Gagné Printing

Published in Canada by
Doubleday Canada Limited
105 Bond Street
Toronto, Ontario
M5B 1Y3

The author wishes to acknowledge the following:

My editor at the *Times-Colonist*, Don Vipond, for letting me take
so much time off to do this book; my father, James, who has hardly
seen anything of me for the past few months; my brother, Nick, who
brewed a few hundred gallons of beer which kept my pen oiled; Mari
Ogawa for teaching me how to use the @*!!#?!* computer; John Pearce,
at Doubleday, who has suffered many sleepless nights wondering if I
would ever finish; Christine Harrison, my editor at Doubleday, who
took an atrocious manuscript and made it readable in record time; my
agent, Denise Bukowski, who would like to strangle me; and the Jack
Daniels distillery for helping me keep all this in the proper perspective.

Thank you.

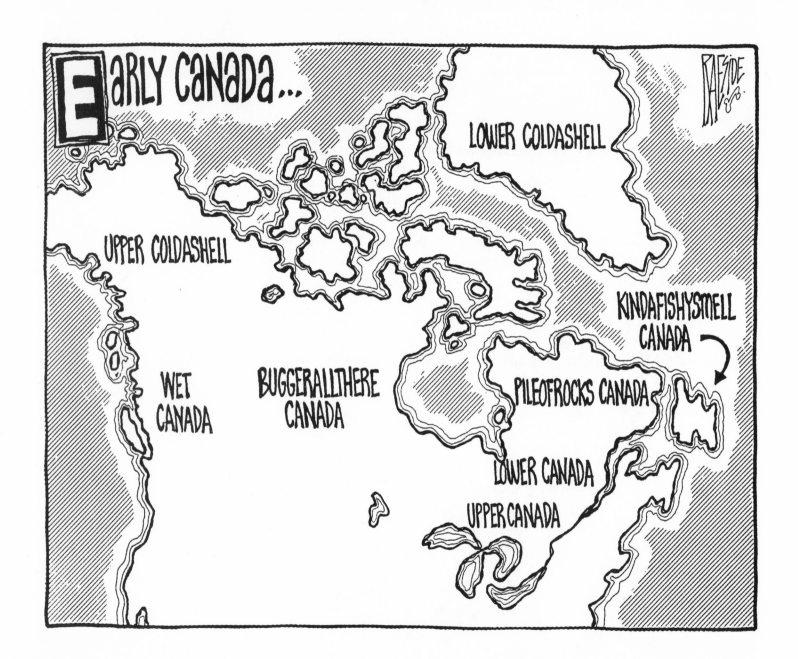

Contents

In the beginning . . .

Chapter 1

A GATHERING OF THIEVES

We may not like to admit it, but we are all boat people. We are reminded of this whenever we see the floating hulks that the latest new immigrants to Canada turn up in (legally or otherwise). Compared to the converted garbage scows our ancestors sailed over on and the conditions they endured, these later forms of transportation are pretty swank. The only non-boat people living in Canada are the native Indians. They cheated – they walked across from Siberia.

Long before the whiteman came, these natives were managing to subsist off the land. Succulent wild berries, grains and fish were supplemented by the odd moose, rabbit, bear or goose. The Indians struggled to maintain a respectable standard of living, one seemingly based on sheer chaos: no taxation system; no parliament (or senate); no convenience stores. One can only guess at their profound gratefulness upon seeing the first Europeans who, surely, would deliver them from such Hell on earth.

The Norsemen were the first Europeans to turn up. They were the first of a long line of navigators who just happened to bump into North America on their way somewhere more financially interesting. (At least we think they were first, based on the remains of their

settlements. It is possible that one day, some archaeologist is going to dig up the relics of a 2,000-year-old Greek lamb bake on P.E.I.) The Norsemen's noble voyages of discovery were not undertaken to spread European Culture, not that there was much of that around in the eleventh century. No, these sea explorers were essentially pirates, out to see what they could help themselves to across the ocean. Considering the size of North America, it seemed inevitable that, before long, some clown would collide with it. Oddly enough, the Norse all thought they had reached India.

Erik the Red was one of the more unpleasant Vikings (mind you, the inhabitants of the various Christian settlements in Europe who had been receiving regular visits from the Vikings would have had a hard time declaring a sole winner in a "Mr Homicidal Maniac 1001" contest.) Erik, however, was even more twisted than his colleagues. When his neighbours asked that he keep the noise down, he packed up his family, his axes and his thumbscrews and sailed off in a big Viking-sized snit. He ended up on the shores of Greenland and promptly set up shop.

One of Erik's companions had a son, Bjorn, who tore himself away from decapitating monks long enough to visit pater in Greenland. Unfortunately, he missed Greenland by a considerable amount and ended up off the coast of North America, which at that time was loaded with trees. Knowing that there weren't any trees in Greenland and if there were, Erik would have probably whacked them down by now, Bjorn paused long enough to disembowel his navigator and retraced his steps to Greenland.

Actually hitting his target this time, Bjorn recounted the story of his heroic navigation and how he had discovered a land covered in big yummy trees, just begging to be cut down and turned into clubs, racks, and spears – all the necessities of Viking life. Erik the Red (now known as Erik the Grey) was getting past all the raping and pillaging, so he sent his son Leif to check out the new spread.

On arrival, Leif and his friends built a settlement. They found a profusion of grape vines growing nearby, so they called the new land "Vineland" – changed the next year to "Chardonnayland."

After a few years of commuting between Greenland and Vineland, the Norsemen became bored with being beaten up by the natives, who weren't as docile as the European Christians. The settlement was abandoned and they returned to Europe to take it out on a couple of monasteries in England.

North America once again belonged to the Indians.

Fast forward to 1497. Lurking in England after Chris Columbus returned from *his* discovery of America (with a few miserable gift-wrapped Indians as proof) was John Cabot. A keen Venetian sailor and keener merchant, Cabot figured that the new continent was in fact the other side of Asia and a quick way to piles of money. Financed by King Henry of England, Cabot loaded up a few beads and a receipt book and tore over to North America. Whether by accident or by design, Cabot found himself anchored off the coast of Newfoundland, staring at a pile of windswept rocks – not quite the subtropical paradise that Columbus had described. After the regulation planting of the flag and claiming a pile of stones for the King of England, his heirs, *et al.*, Cabot sailed further north, and got really depressed. There was bugger-all up north and the European markets were already flooded with that.

Cabot, however, did drop a line overboard and was astounded at the fishing. Although the voyage didn't make him wealthy, he saved his neck from Henry's chopping block with all the fish he brought back. Soon, there was a regular shuttle service of boats sailing over from Europe to help themselves to anything with fins. Not too different from today.

Hot on the heels of Britain's Cabot came Jacques Cartier. Either fuelled by that peculiar habit of the French to one-up the English, or a desire to save the new world from bad English cooking, Cartier set sail from France to explore what had now been named America, after the Italian explorer Amerigo Vespucci. (Columbus was obviously not as savvy when it came to PR otherwise he might have named it "Columba".) Cartier was not the only explorer heading to America. The Atlantic ocean in the 1500s was swarming with ships of all sizes, all determined to claim a piece of the new land for whatever King or Queen they were trying to curry favour with at the time. Most of these

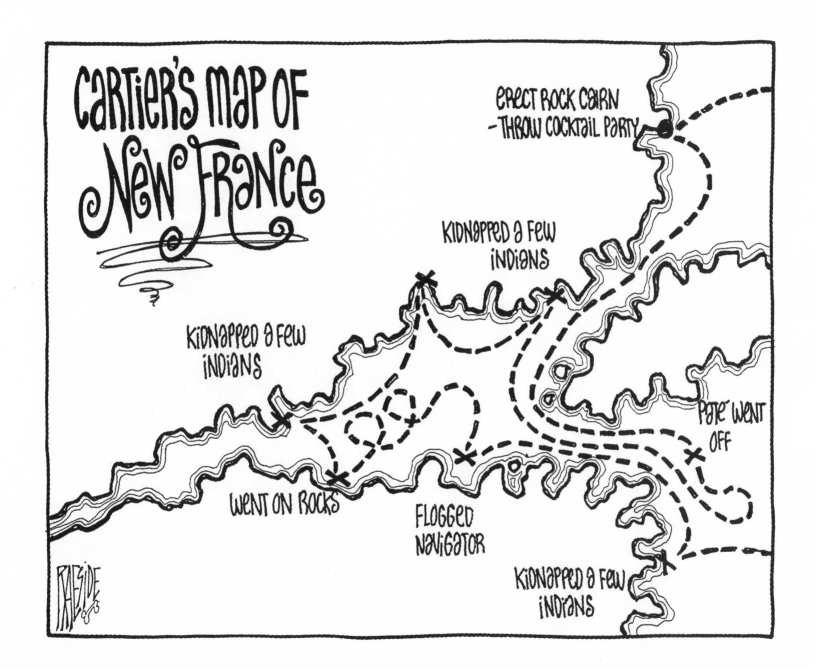

explorers were on their way to find a round *around* America. Everyone was looking for the East Indies, Asia or India and hadn't twigged that America literally split the globe in half. Cartier too figured there might be a route through America, a river, *n'est-ce pas*? A tunnel? Reaching the Gulf of St. Lawrence, Cartier squeezed past the dozens of Europeans who were slaughtering cod by the thousands and headed west, up the north shore. The landscape was pretty uninspiring and they ran out of Châteauneuf-du-Pape '31. In disgust, he headed for home.

Cartier returned better prepared the next year, armed with an extra 25 cases of a rather delicious Burgundy. Arriving in the Gulf again, Cartier took on two native guides, slapped them around, paid them minimum wage and proceeded again up the St. Lawrence, stopping occasionally to set up monuments to the King of France. A few miles up the river, Cartier had forgotten all about finding a route to Asia; he was salivating from local tales of heaps of gold and silver waiting up the river. Winter set in before they had filled their pockets, so Cartier's sailors built a stockade and settled in for what they thought would be a pleasant winter holiday. Instead, they were attacked by cold, scurvy and Indians.

Cartier returned to France that spring without treasure but with a few cold and seasick Indians as gifts. This was not unusual for that period, as Columbus had begun what was now a roaring trade across the Atlantic in kidnapped natives. Back in France, Cartier was the darling of the court and lounged about milking his celebrity status for six years before he went back to America. The captured natives did not return with him as they died soon after arriving in France (possibly poisoned from a bad bottle of Beaujolais Superieur, but more likely starved to death in the basement of the royal horse barn). Cartier brought back with him farmers, colonists, tools and enough brandy to ward off the rigours of another Canadian winter. Things had changed in Cartier's absence. The natives, still a little ticked off at the suspicious disappearance of six of their mates when J.C. was there last time had it in for him and were downright rude to the settlers. After another cold winter the settlers skulked back onto their ships. Hurling the last empty claret bottle in the direction of the native village, Cartier left for France, never to return.

The English were more than a little annoyed to hear of Cartier's efforts to colonize what the French had now named New France. After all, it *was* John Cabot who had initially discovered the new continent,

and what were those disgusting, garlic-eating Frenchmen doing on what was destined eventually to become a private hunting preserve for idle English noblemen? In order to strengthen England's claim on Canada, five ships were sent out under the command of Sir Humphrey Gilbert, a pal of the Queen. They had a pretty successful journey, as British explorations go: one boat turned back after two days because the crew were seasick; the remaining four were thrashed for seven weeks by Atlantic storms; half the crew of one boat were drowned while looting a fishing boat. Of the remaining three boats, one hit a sandbank and sank, while the other two sailed for home, encountering the same idyllic conditions as on the voyage out. Only one made it home to England, the other sank, taking the intrepid Sir Humphrey with it.

By now, most explorers had figured out that Asia was on the other side of America and had found a way around the southern tip of the continent. Only one problem – it was a hell of a long way via that route. A conglomerate of English traders whined to the court that a shorter route must quickly be found across the top of Canada, or their profits might plunge from 3,000% to 2,950%. Another intrepid English sailor, Martin Frobisher, was commissioned. Frobisher sailed until he found the coast of America, turned hard right and headed north. Shivering in their boots and dodging icebergs, Frobisher's crew were convinced they would sight China any day. Unfortunately, they plowed into the ice while still off the east coast of Canada. On his trip home, Frobisher took a wrong turn at an iceberg and spent the next three months trying to find his way back to England. The only bright part of this fiasco occurred when an Indian gave him a small black rock covered in little gold sparkly bits. Frobisher stuffed it in his pocket and forgot about it until he got home, where an observant geologist pointed out that it was loaded with gold. The lure of gold proved

quite an advantage when trying to recruit crew for future expeditions to find the Northwest Passage. Usually discretely omitted from English history textbooks, these forays were notable only for their spectacular failures.

It wasn't long before explorers stumbled on another form of gold – furs. (Attached to four legs and infinitely easier to find.) The natives seemed delighted to trade furs, of which they had plenty, for bits of metal and glass, of which they had none. French explorers were first, and the settlers were not far behind. Soon everyone was in the act and the Indians were mowing down anything with hair on it to feed the demand. Ships returning to Europe almost sank under the weight of furs, while those leaving France had holds crammed with cheap rubbish. Eventually, the natives got tired of the garbage that was being fobbed off on them and demanded better. Guns would be nice, maybe a little gunpowder, possibly a bullet or two? Although swapping weapons for furs was officially forbidden, traders were only too happy to oblige, giving the natives a little more muscle in future negotiations with the French. The Northern Inuit were the first to try out their new weapons, massacring a few fur traders. No one seemed to mind too much, so long as it was the other guy being terminated. It wasn't long before everything with four legs and fur was being wiped out. The Hurons were the worst offenders and were soon reduced to buying beaver pelts from other tribes in an effort to keep their customers satisfied. Considering the wholesale slaughter, it's amazing that there is anything left to put on our coins.

The French rep. in New France was now Samuel de Champlain (draftsman, geographer and smartly-dressed explorer). He made a number of trips to poke around New France, beginning in 1603. Champlain celebrated his latest return by shooting a few Iroquois. The Iroquois, whom the French settlers were doing their best to exterminate, were fierce fighters and seemed thoroughly to enjoy scalping and impaling the white settlers as fast as they could get their hands on them. Champlain had been stirring the pot, allying with the Hurons, who were not on speaking terms with the Iroquois. Champlain supplied guns to the Hurons, who pointed them in the direction of their enemies.

In the spring of 1629, just as the settlers were starting to get it together, the Kirke brothers, a couple of English privateers (pirates) sailed up the St. Lawrence, anchored off the poorly defended town of Quebec, trained their guns on Phillipe's Bistro & Café and said, "Hand it

over, *garçon.*" Undefended Quebec surrendered and the French were shown the door. The Kirkes immediately fell about stripping anything that wasn't nailed down. By the time a treaty was signed in 1632 and New France was returned to the French, most of the town of Quebec was either in the Kirkes' front parlour in Ipswich, or had been tossed into the St. Lawrence.

The British had also been busy during this period. Firmly entrenched in the Maritimes, they were happily slaughtering whales by the thousands. "Canada," as the land had come to be known, was still thought of as just an awkward pile of rocks keeping explorers from easy access to all those lovely Eastern silks and spices. (The origin of the word "Canada" is unclear, but there is speculation it derives from a little-known Indian word roughly translated to mean "please exploit me.") Back in 1610, King James, on the lookout for a new wardrobe, had dispatched skilled navigator Henry Hudson to find the rumoured North West Passage. Predictably, the expedition was a spectacular failure and Hudson ended up frozen in ice for the winter. What made him special was that he got further than anyone else (Hudson's Bay) and his crew mutinied, pushing him off in a small boat with some of his officers, a case of salt pork and a street map of Liverpool.

After eyeing French ships groaning under the weight of tons of furs passing by their Maritime outposts, on their way to decorating the bidets of the French court, the British thought they'd dabble in the fur business themselves. With the French monopolizing the south east, Charles II authorized the Hudson's Bay Company, founded by the King's cousin and a few of his foppish boyfriends, to set up shop in northern Canada. The Company commissioned the *Nonsuch* and sent her to Hudson's Bay for a little exploratory pillaging. The *Nonsuch* returned awash with beaver pelts. Ecstatic at the thought of huge profits, the company set up its first permanent trading post at Moose Factory. (Although there is no record of any moose ever being processed there.) Hedging its bets on future expansion, the HBC laid claim to the rest of Canada. (The French, needless to say, were somewhat miffed to lose their lucrative monopoly on muff sales.) The English weren't as fussy as the French about trading guns and booze with the natives. With any luck, they reasoned, the natives might celebrate a good sale by getting squiffy and shooting a few Frenchmen.

French traders, fearing they might end up like the Canadian beaver, sneaked overland and captured some northern British outposts. The British retaliated by capturing some southern French outposts. This tit-for-tatting came to an end in 1686 with the signing of the Treaty Of Neutrality between Louis XIV (whose wardrobe was stuffed with outrageous beaver outfits) and James II. The treaty guaranteed peace in America, despite the usual butchery taking place in Europe – an early example of profit taking precedence over pride. Like most treaties of that era, it didn't last long. Four years later, the British navy was back, lobbing cannon balls into Quebec City.

Not content with just exploiting the natives financially, both the French and the English shamefully took advantage of intertribal rivalry. The French wined and dined the Hurons and Ojibwa. The English became chums with the Iroquois and Mohawks. Neither the French nor the English had the slightest qualms about setting the Indians onto rival European settlements. Every massacre was avenged with two others. Every barbaric act was an excuse to do something even more unspeakable. The natives were delighted that their talents were in such demand and were quick learners when it came to picking up the finer points of European barbarism.

Unfortunately, many of the victims were women and children, whose lives were tough enough fighting off starvation, disease and cold, without the added burden of Indian bounty hunters trying to fill their daily quota. Fearless warriors when armed with traditional weapons, the natives became almost invincible when they started carrying muskets and knives. The only things stopping them were the diseases brought over from Europe.

Disease was spreading rapidly: smallpox, scurvy, dysentery, cholera, typhus, rheumatic fever, along with poor diet and lousy sanitation contributed to wiping out hundreds of settlers every winter. It was the natives who got the worst of it. With no natural immunities, whole tribes were wiped out. Just the sniffles could kill them.

Disease and discomfort were exactly what the French missionaries were looking for. They joined the settlers, bringing with them the word of God, a rigid form of religious government and a few new diseases. The natives preferred staying "uncivilized." Being uncivilized meant you didn't have to say "sorry" every time you whipped off someone's scalp. It wasn't long before the Indians carved up a couple of priests, a friendly hint to the missionaries to cool their organizational fervour.

By 1755 the English were doing housecleaning, rounding up some of the French-speaking Acadians in Nova Scotia, herding them onto boats and shipping them back to France. Unfortunately, a couple of ships sank, taking some of the 12,000 Acadians with them. The English "tut tutted" and "what a shamed," while the French, understandably ticked off, raided a couple of English forts. As the English had flung the French out of Nova Scotia earlier, the English got booted out of their fort on Lake Ontario, and so on. The loss of the French fortress Louisbourg on Isle Royal was the last straw. In 1759, the Marquis de Montcalm, commander of French forces in North America, sent a frantic message back

to France, appealing for help before the British overran them. However, things weren't going too well for the French in Europe either, so Montcalm was on his own. Montcalm (to the chagrin of skinny, port-soaked General Wolfe, commander of British forces in North America) refused to take a stand for the final, decisive battle for control of New France; he retreated to Quebec City. Montcalm and Co. hunkered down on the cliffs around the city, which not only gave them a swell view, but also a good position to shoot anything that moved below. The British forces obliged them by doing an awful lot of moving – up the cliff. The French simply sat at the top, waited until the British stuck their noses over, then pinged them off. Wolfe, from the Lemming School of Military Tactics and preoccupied with an embarrassing case of dysentery, sent hundreds of British soldiers up the cliffs, only to have them fall back to the beach full of French holes. Wolfe retired to his bed in a snit, accompanied by a case of port and a case of piles.

Wolfe had to take Quebec, or he'd never get his ships up the St. Lawrence. If he didn't attack the French soon, the ships would have to

go back to England in disgrace. Supplies were at an end, everyone had dysentery and winter was drawing near. In the dead of night, Wolfe sent his soldiers up the river and past the French sentries, to ascend to the Plains of Abraham, dragging cannons, ammunition and a couple of cases of Kaopectate behind them. Montcalm's forces were hiding in the lowlands giggling up their sleeves, expecting the English attack to come from a different direction. Montcalm didn't believe his scouts who'd told him the entire British army were strolling about picking wildflowers on the Plains of Abraham. Wolfe wasn't a heck of a lot more brilliant, setting up on low ground, waiting for the French attack to come from another direction. Eventually both sides found each other and proceeded to do what armies do best – kill. The French defence included a large number of poorly-trained militia, who were mown down at close range by lines of well-trained British musketeers. The battle didn't last long, just long enough for Wolfe to get shot twice and Montcalm once. Both died that day, along with hundreds of other soldiers who, unlike their brilliant commanding officers, didn't have their passing immortalized in numerous impossibly romantic paintings. Naturally – at least in English history books – Wolfe was hailed as a genius and Montcalm went down in history as a bum. But if Montcalm hadn't been just as much of a tactical twit as Wolfe, the attack would have been written up in that jumbo 200-volume set, *British Military Blunders*.

It wasn't long before the French launched a counterattack against the British at Quebec, but apart from creating a dozen more widows and reducing a couple of churches to gravel, no real estate changed hands. The British sailed on past Quebec, helping themselves to Montreal and what is now Toronto, pausing only to burn down houses of anyone not prominently displaying portraits of King George (available for 2s/6d from the Royal Navy Commissary in Quebec City).

In a retaliatory move, a French task force, made up of four warships and 700 men, sailed into St. John's harbour in Newfoundland and captured the British fort. Back in France, King Louis hailed it a brilliant military victory and declared that British domination of New France was coming to a sticky end. (The British defence at St. John 's consisted of 60 soldiers, three cooks, a janitor and a cat named Simon.)

Three months later, the British sent over their own warships and booted the French out. Back in France, King Louis declared it shithouse luck.

Picking their way out of the rubble of what was left of New France, there wasn't much left for the French to do but surrender unconditionally, and in 1763, France signed the Treaty of Paris, handing over what was left of New France to Britain. Spain, which was also on the outs, threw in Florida at the same time. The English found themselves in possession of most of North America.

Only one small detail prevented the British from sending over boatloads of tourists to stroll the romantic cobbled streets of Quebec: the Ojibwa. Hundreds of them. It appeared no one had bothered to tell them the war was over. After getting bashed around for a few months, the British made a peace of sorts with Pontiac and the Ojibwa, and set up the first reservations. Having segregated the natives into crowded quarters, the Brits rewarded themselves with spacious fertile areas on which to build forts and barricades to keep an eye on their enemies.

Several centuries of Canadian history came to a close. The French were glowering at the British, the British were eyeing the French, and no one had bothered to pay the native landlords for the battle-scarred turf.

Chapter 2

RAPING 'N' PILLAGING

It wasn't long before the scourge of modern society slithered down the gangplank of a ship from England: bureaucrats, swarms of them, finding a fertile feeding ground among the unorganized settlers. One of the first things they did was set up the Quebec Act, which gave the province of Quebec control over all of British North America, thus guaranteeing themselves and their descendants jobs for life. A system of government based on the old authoritarian French–Roman Catholic system was set up, spoiling everyone's fun. Up to then, settlers in the colonies did as they pleased, without interference from governments who were preoccupied fighting amongst themselves in Europe. Now that there was peace in Europe for more than a two-day period, the British government turned its attention in Canada on how to pay for the last, very expensive hundred years of war. They'd wrung everything out of the starving population at home, so attention turned to the North American settlers. The French act (which was the model for Revenue Canada), meant taxes, tithes, taxes and taxes for the colonists, who had left Europe to escape that misery in the first place. (The British government would have introduced a GST in the eighteenth century, had they thought of it.)

By 1775, taxes, and demands for limited self-government, had
turned British colonies in the south into a writhing mass of discontent.
Capitalizing on this hatred was that old slaver himself, George Washington and a few of his mates, Ben Franklin and Ben Arnold among them.
Declaring independence from Britain, they raided a British fort with a
force of renegade soldiers led by Ben Arnold. Chuffed by their success,
the American Minutemen – as they called themselves – turned up
in Quebec to finish the British off. Floundering through deep snow-
drifts, the Minutemen were able to capture undefended Montreal.
The Americans were just as surprised as the Brits were, finding themselves wandering about the streets of Montreal, virtually unopposed.
It wasn't quite the same when Arnie and his pals wandered a little
further downstream to Quebec City, where a force was waiting for
them, made up of British soldiers, Newfie fishermen, sailors, a few
housewives armed with rolling pins and the British governor. After
enduring a few hours of concentrated clobbering, the Americans
retreated in disarray, leaving behind most of their soldiers with either
holes in them, or frostbite. The British were ecstatic and proclaimed it a
display of military genius. While the American rebels stumbled about
helplessly in the snow outside, British officers relaxed in front of
roaring fires in toasty warm officers' messes, guzzling port, ordering
new medals and attending the occasional execution. Fortunately for
the Americans, they had better success in the snow-free south, relieving the British of the burden of ownership of Fort Ticonderoga and
Bunker Hill. The British government called them cowardly sneak
attacks by ungrateful traitors.

The Americans were helped enormously in their battle for independence, by the fact that the King of England, George III, was
absolutely, barking mad. Not the usual endearing inbred dottiness that

the English were used to, but a real wacko lunacy that made it difficult for British generals to carry out military operations in the colonies.

Besides, the American rebels weren't playing fair, hiding in bushes and ambushing smart files of British Redcoats. Naturally, the Redcoats could be spotted miles away and made tempting targets for the ragtag group of farmers who made up the Continental army. American privateers were having a field day sinking British supply ships. Pirates from all over the world suddenly found within themselves fierce patriotic pride and were only too happy to fly an American flag while going about their usual thuggery. Occasionally they would make a mistake and shoot an American ship, but in the days before concealed camcorders and marking valuables with your driver's licence number, it was hard to prove who did what and to whom. Meanwhile, King George was having a pillow fight with Robert and Marion, two of his favourite hunting dogs.

The war was going badly for the loyal colonists (one assumes they *enjoyed* being taxed into extinction) who found themselves in the middle of the fight. Many packed up their T-4s and sneaked up into Canada, which had so far remained firmly under British control, despite Ben Franklin's generous offer to annex the country. The French allied with the Americans and took the opportunity to settle a few old scores. The British finally conceded that the American colonies were lost and withdrew to Canada with their tails between their legs. King George, when informed of the loss of the colonies barked like a dog for two hours then retired to Balmoral, to take it out on 2,407 grouse, 423 pheasants, a cow and two gamekeepers.

After the loss of the American colonies, thousands of Loyalist settlers poured across the border, stripped of their land by the Americans and not feeling well-disposed toward the government that had let them down. The British, more out of fear of what thousands of unhappy, well-armed refugees could do to a demoralized British garrison, than out of generosity, guaranteed land to those who had been loyal to the crown throughout the war. Among those who took them up on the offer were a few thousand Negroes who had fought on the British side. They were presented with a barren rock-strewn moonscape in Nova Scotia, while their white comrades-in-arms were settling comfortably into their free farms in fertile Upper Canada. (Upper Canada was southern Ontario. Lower Canada comprised much of Quebec, including Montreal and Quebec City. It was no wonder the

British couldn't find the Northwest Passage). The distribution of free land, implements, seeds and leisure footwear to the loyalists was a sore point to the existing settlers who had to scratch about on their own, without government freebies. Needless to say, everyone took out their frustrations on the black settlers. Meanwhile, King George was waltzing naked on the roof of the west wing of Blenheim Palace, with an ostrich named Judy.

The British were relieved to see the end of the eighteenth century. They had lost the American colonies, Canada was teeming with unhappy loyalists and ace English explorer, Captain Cook had been chopped into salami on the Sandwich Islands. Traditionally, English explorers were of the invincible type: strong jaws, big shirts, nifty hats; they were darlings of the courts. Only occasionally did they drown, freeze or become snacks for wild animals. They weren't supposed to be massacred.

Captain Cook had done a sterling job of spreading British interests and diseases around the globe, including Hawaii, the west coast of North America, New Zealand and dozens of fly-blown islands in between. Naturally, all his firsts were disputed by everyone from the Dutch to the Spanish. But in the days before McDonald's and Burger King, it was hard to leave a permanent cultural mark on new territories. Cairns erected by explorers could be torn down in a rage by the next expedition, or turned into a barbeque pit by the natives in preparation for the next explorer.

There is no doubt, however, that Spanish explorer Galiano was the first European to discover the west coast of North America. The Spanish had been roaming South America and the California coast for quite some time. By now, everyone had given up on trying to find the Northwest Passage except the British, who, on hearing of Cook's discoveries immediately launched expeditions to locate the Northwest Passage from the west. Initial west to east attempts were as successful as the east to west disasters had been. Hot on the heels of the explorers came the British merchants who arrived with the usual cheap beads and threats, relieving the natives of their furs, minerals and anything else that could be resold at a profit back home.

The discovery of the West Coast came just in time, as natural resources in the interior weren't reproducing fast enough to keep up with demand; it was time to start fresh out west. The Spanish, noticing the large numbers of English ships sailing past their California villas loaded with furs, sent an expedition up to Nootka Sound to get rid of the poachers. The Spanish, who piously claimed they had settled the west coast of America solely to bring Catholicism to the area, were also peeved to see Church of England missionaries busily initiating the natives to *their* brand of Christianity in exchange for muskets and powder. It would have taken the exchange of superior firepower for the Spanish to convert them back.

Britain realized that exploitation of the West Coast would have to be exclusively by ship, as no overland route had yet been hacked out. So they sent George Vancouver, one of their few naval captains who hadn't been slaughtered by the French. Cap'n George was to assist the pillaging by making accurate coastal charts of anything hard that might sink ships and cut into profits. He was also to find any rivers leading inland that might be navigable by barges. Sailing past the Columbia River into the Strait of Georgia and completely missing the Fraser River,

Vancouver returned home declaring there was no way to reach the east from the west. Unfortunately for him, another explorer, Alexander Mackenzie, *did* reach the west by a rather tortuous overland route, but came to the conclusion that the route was unsuitable for commerce. It wasn't until 1808 that another explorer, Simon Fraser, actually made it down the Fraser River in a canoe. The Prairies, home to the engaging and hospitable Plains Indians, were just as difficult to reach. Between Montreal and Lake Superior were no less than 36 portages. (No wonder that word stuck when people got around to naming Winnipeg's dusty streets.)

Back East, relations between Americans and British had been decidedly chilly since the last British Redcoat slunk out of the colonies. The British had kept the feud fresh by taking every opportunity to lord their naval superiority over any American ships they came across. The Brits had resorted to the same tactics the Americans used during the war and hired back the privateers to harass American ships on a bounty system. The British used the excuse that as Napoleon was blockading Britain and the Americans were allied to the French, it was fair game. The Americans, new to the intricacies of world diplomacy, declared war on Canada on June 19, 1812 and immediately lost Detroit to the British. (There are many in the US today who wish the British had kept Detroit so the Brits now would be stuck with the blame every time a Detroit-made car falls apart on the freeway.)

The British garrison was on its own when it came to fighting the Americans, as British troops in Europe were preoccupied with Napoleon's rampages. Besides, even if there had been troops to spare, the French had the British navy bottled up, and the Atlantic wasn't the healthiest place for any ships flying the red ensign.

For two years battles raged back and forth across the border; Washington sacked by the British, York sacked by the Americans. . . . It was

The Canada - U.S. border - 1812

INDIANS SELL OUT TO THE AMERICANS...

LAURA SECORD PLAYS WATCHDOG...

AMERICANS ATTACK ON A BANK HOLIDAY...

INDIANS SELL OUT TO THE BRITISH...

COMMUNICATIONS PROBLEMS...

IT WAS MONDAY...

hard sometimes to define where the border was; it was moved every week, depending on who won the last skirmish. Settlers were getting tired of constantly packing up their belongings and moving along with their loyalties. Most of the battles were lost either through sheer incompetence or won through pure luck. The war became so confusing that even the British, who loved nothing more than a damned good fight, were losing interest. On Christmas Eve 1814, the Americans and British signed a peace treaty. Although all occupied lands were returned to their former owners, minus a few buildings, no agreement was made concerning the location of a new border. This was handy, as it left open the threat of occasional military action, which could lead to more medals all round. One of the more notorious trouble spots was the Pacific coast, which the Americans and British governed jointly, until an independent tribunal could sort the whole mess out.

At this point, Britain had established in Canada an efficient bureaucracy, defended it from American invasion, set up branch offices out west, and, through a raft of new taxes, had guaranteed their perpetuity.

Chapter 3

DIVIDING THE SPOILS

Around the time the Canadian governor and his mates were tucking into their twenty-third celebratory cask of port, mumblings of internal dissent began against what was essentially a military dictatorship/big business/old boys' club running the show. The North West Company, who were competing with the Hudson's Bay Company to see who could screw the largest number of natives out of the largest number of furs, were being harassed by the native Métis population who inhabited the rich prairie lands beside the Red River. Descendants of trysts between French *voyageurs* and natives, the Métis were steamed by the high-handed actions of the North West Company in setting up the Red River colony in their backyard. The NWC felt the best way to help the situation would be to even the odds. To that end, they shipped over Scottish crofters who had been turfed out of their homes during the Highland Clearances and had become Europe's bag ladies. But a few weeks after they turned up in Red River, the Scots disappeared. Rumours were rife that the HBC was inciting the Métis to make life awkward for its chief rival.

In order to restore order, the NWC sent out a hit man, Lord Selkirk, who together with a bunch of ex-soldiers from the War of 1812 blew

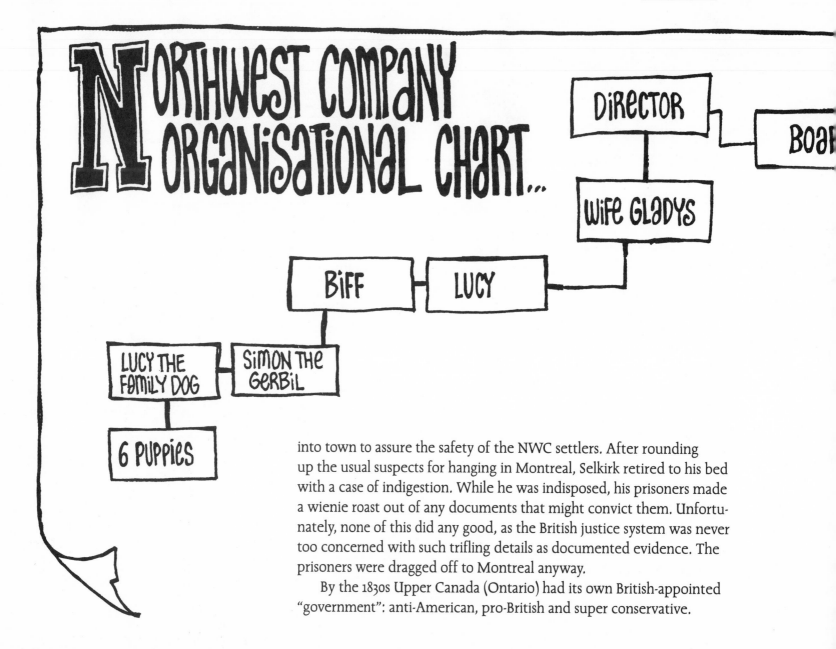

Northwest Company Organisational Chart...

DIRECTOR

WIFE GLADYS

BOAR[D]

BIFF

LUCY

LUCY THE FAMILY DOG

SIMON THE GERBIL

6 PUPPIES

into town to assure the safety of the NWC settlers. After rounding up the usual suspects for hanging in Montreal, Selkirk retired to his bed with a case of indigestion. While he was indisposed, his prisoners made a wienie roast out of any documents that might convict them. Unfortunately, none of this did any good, as the British justice system was never too concerned with such trifling details as documented evidence. The prisoners were dragged off to Montreal anyway.

By the 1830s Upper Canada (Ontario) had its own British-appointed "government": anti-American, pro-British and super conservative.

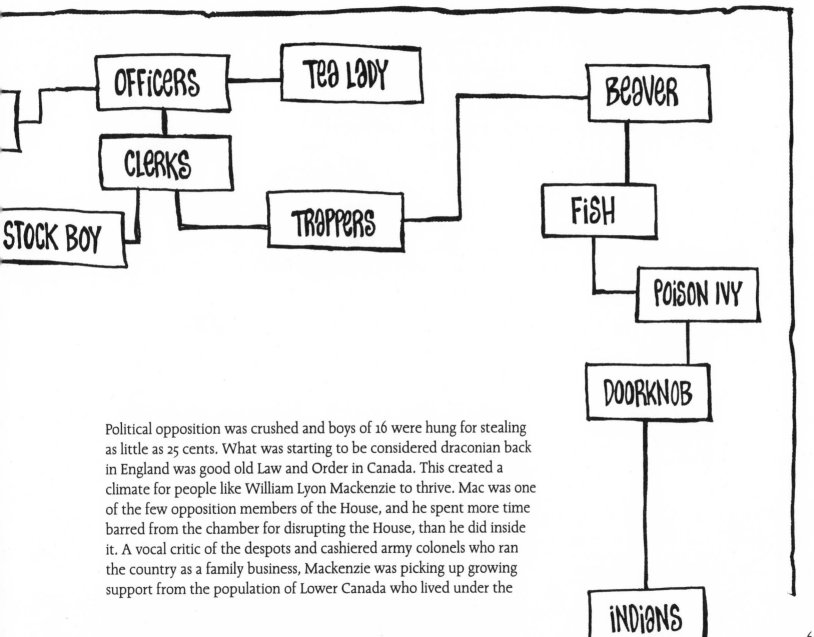

OFFICERS

TEA LADY

BEAVER

CLERKS

STOCK BOY

TRAPPERS

FISH

POISON IVY

DOORKNOB

INDIANS

Political opposition was crushed and boys of 16 were hung for stealing as little as 25 cents. What was starting to be considered draconian back in England was good old Law and Order in Canada. This created a climate for people like William Lyon Mackenzie to thrive. Mac was one of the few opposition members of the House, and he spent more time barred from the chamber for disrupting the House, than he did inside it. A vocal critic of the despots and cashiered army colonels who ran the country as a family business, Mackenzie was picking up growing support from the population of Lower Canada who lived under the constant threat of being hung for sedition or of dying from cholera. Although slavery had been officially abolished throughout the British Empire, racial attitudes had hardened under the Conservative government and the once acceptable marriages between natives and settlers were now considered "improper" and "revolting." Of course, sexual liaisons between British officers and Indian women was still "good sport." The rebels were made up of Canadians who were fed up with being pushed around by crown-appointed, rather than elected officials.

On December 5, 1837 the long simmering Rebellion began. Led by Mackenzie, the newly formed patriot rebels never stood a chance. Armed with pitchforks and outdated muskets, they were cut to pieces by British troops. True to grand old British traditions, the wounded were bayonetted and the survivors were executed at invitation-only hangings. Mackenzie fled to the US – perhaps to stock up on cheaper, Buffalo-area bayonets.

Even though the revolt was crushed, the British government couldn't ignore the fact that they might have another War of Independence on their hands. To head off the possibility, British colonial officials introduced the Act of Union which united Upper and Lower Canada. Appointees would no longer be able to hold their positions for life. This was a radical step towards an elected government. Kingston was designated the capital of Canada and the first legislature opened June 14, 1841.

One would be hard pressed to call it a parliament, as the governor general, Charles Thomson, had stacked the building to the rafters with his own supporters and various other Tory thugs, making it the forerunner of today's Senate. (In fact, some of those people may still be in today's Senate.) Needless to say, no reformist legislation was allowed past the front door. Canada remained mired in a Conservative time

warp even after Parliament moved to sexier Montreal, where MPs could indulge more fully in their respective vices.

Meanwhile, the British obsession with the Northwest Passage was still going strong, and the crew of expedition #12,459 to find the Passage were locked in the Arctic ice shivering in their regulation British Navy issue tropical shorts. London newspapers were filled with lurid accounts of expeditions, accompanied by heroic etchings of explorers strolling about the ice in tophats and tails. In reality, the explorers had long ago eaten their gear and were now eyeing each other as potential dishes *du jour*. Although the British public and Canadian settlers took a keen interest in their exploits, no one had the foggiest idea where places like Fort Enterprise or Moose Factory were. Canada's North was like the moon or Mars is to us today, a great place to get to first and colour red on the map, but not really suitable for lounging about in wicker chairs and ordering smart gin and tonics. As well, spices from the Orient that had seemed so important 60 years before, had become redundant as British cuisine improved. (A debatable point if you've ever eaten in a British pub recently.) Notwithstanding, Sir John Franklin set out again in 1845 (for the third and last time) to find the elusive Passage. Later, an expedition was launched to find the Franklin expedition.

Over on the West Coast, despite the trifling detail that the land wasn't theirs, the British government handed Vancouver Island over to the Hudson's Bay Company in 1849. This was to prevent the island being overrun by American settlers or runaway slaves moving North. In exchange for the land, the HBC would have to colonize the area with politically correct settlers as quickly as possible. Wanting to be fair, James Douglas, HBC's factor for the coast, bought the island from the natives for 371 cheap blankets and a cap reading "I left my land with the Hudson's Bay Co." This magnanimous approach was by no means

restricted to the coast. All over Canada Indian tribes were being relieved of their land in exchange for lousy blankets, obsolete muskets, glass beads, cheap booze, venereal diseases and a knock on the head.

Runaway Negro slaves began crossing the border into Canada, as the US Civil War began raging in 1861. Their exodus would have come as no surprise to anyone who had read Harriet Beecher Stowe's novel entitled *Uncle Tom's Cabin*. The book chronicled the cruelties suffered by the Negroes at the hands of their masters. No one believed H.B.S's claims, until first-hand accounts made the book's accounts seem like an excerpt from a Sunday-school reading.

The Seigneurial system, one of the last bastions of early French oppression in Quebec, had been abolished in 1854. *Seigneurs*, moronic noblemen and cashiered military officers had been given tracts of land, along with resident peasants (*habitants*) to do with as they pleased. The new legislation wasn't that sweeping; communities were required to compensate the *seigneurs* for the land they lost. Most *habitants* felt it was a small price to pay to rid themselves of parasites and gain control of their lives.

April 12, 1851 had seen the introduction of Canada Post, and the first letter mailed in Canada using the 3d. first-class stamp. On June 16, 1964, the letter was delivered. April 13, 1851 marked the introduction of the first rate increase, followed by the first postal strike on the 14th.

In 1855, the capital of Canada, which had been bounced around a

bit, landed in Toronto, for what was promised to be the last time. It was moved to Ottawa two years later. In order to speed up news from Europe, which had up to now been taking days by ship, a transatlantic telegraph line was laid between the two continents. On both sides of the Atlantic engineers were working day and night to iron out the bugs in the most important link in the cable – the billing procedure.

With the introduction of new technology, more efficient ships, and railways, those who made their living exploiting Canada's flora and fauna could slaughter and chop faster and more efficiently. Whole species of wildlife were now endangered, including Great Auks, whales, and bison. Harp seals were being pick-axed into extinction and the last beaver were hiding out in a duck pond outside of Dryden, Ontario. Somewhere in the R&D Division of Nigel Chainsaw's Axe and Machete factory, an engineer was dreaming up a machine that would send Douglas fir trees the way of the passenger pigeon.

As a welcome balance to the incredible changes in eastern Canada, gold was discovered in British Columbia. Those who weren't already slogging through the mud in the California goldfields were soon taking whatever transportation they could find out to B.C. (Any excuse to get away from the farm, factory, wife and kids.) Ninety-nine-point-nine % of them didn't make a nickel. They had to resort to stealing from those who did, or else set up business selling supplies at outrageous markups.

Meanwhile, in the jointly governed San Juan Islands on the West

Coast, war was about to break out after a British pig was shot after wandering into an American vegetable garden. The British demanded compensation, the Americans demanded applesauce.

There had never been a lack of targets for British soldiers in Canada to shoot at: the French, natives, Americans, reformers, the list goes on. In 1866, just as the British army was studying the want ads for places with more possibilities for medals and looting, a bunch of Irishmen in a pub south of the border drank more than was good for them and invaded Canada. The idea was to capture the country and hold it for ransom, demanding the British get out of Ireland in exchange. This proved a brilliant and cunning plan, except that they were outnumbered 100 to 1 and had only enough Guinness Stout for two days. The coup failed and the lads retreated across the border leaving behind a trail of empties. Meanwhile in the lounge of the Empire Club in Toronto, a piece of the Franklin Expedition was discovered in a gin and tonic, frozen inside an ice cube.

Finally, Canada was starting to take shape as a real nation. A border had been drawn to separate our southern neighbours from us, and new borders had been drawn internally. With Confederation looming, and the beginning of institutions like Canada Post and the Senate, how could the union *not* succeed?

Chapter 4

MORE RAPING 'N' PILLAGING

In 1867 Canada had a new prime minister, John A. Macdonald – hero of the people and darling of the distillers. John A.'s first act was to sail over to England and in between visits to the Rose & Crown and Jolly Miller, grovel at the feet of Queen Victoria, asking if Canada could have her Joan Henry on a mildewed piece of paper called the British North America Act. The Act would give Canada the right to form a dominion of states, made up of four provinces and governed by one central body. (No prizes for guessing who that body would be and who would be running it.) Besides, the British parliament would still have a say if anything radical was proposed.

The original confederation took effect July 1, 1867. The Maritimes proved reluctant, but Nova Scotia and New Brunswick did join the party (Newfoundland held out until 1949.) Now that Canada had a constitution (sort of) she needed a new building to display it in. By an extraordinary coincidence, work had started on the Ottawa parliament buildings a few years before. Only snag was the actual BNA Act stayed in London, as the Queen was concerned that Johnny Macdonald might flog it for a bottle of Johnnie Walker if he was caught short.

The Maritime colonies, although the first discovered and settled, were the last to consider joining the rest of Canada, either as a union of colonies or, as had been suggested, a loose confederation. With large populations of ex-slaves, ex-Americans and Scots, they were highly suspicious of anything that might restrict their independence. Trade within the Maritime communities was based largely on the barter system, which made it extremely difficult for Britain to collect taxes.

In order to lure Prince Edward Island into confederation, the Feds made all sorts of sweetheart deals: offers to pay off their debts,

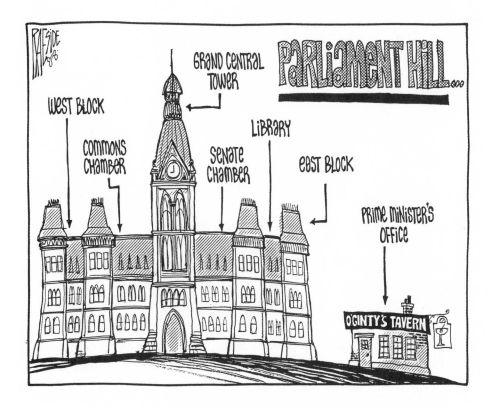

money to operate their legislature, train service to the mainland (a novel idea, considering P.E.I. is obviously an island), two victrolas and a black velvet painting of Queen Victoria. P.E.I. seriously considered the offers, but held out for six more years.

Out west, the Métis, under Louis Riel, hadn't been loafing. They'd been busy giving the Hudson's Bay Company the cold shoulder and declaring a provisional government in Rupert's Land, a region which stretched from Lake Superior up to the Arctic Ocean and as far west as the Rockies. Technically the land belonged to the Métis and local natives. The HBC had inherited it from the North West Company, but the NWC had never bothered buying it from the natives or Métis, and now the HBC was about to transfer ownership to Canada. The US government as well as the US Fenians were also keenly interested in the area, as any internal unrest meant they stood a chance of being invited in to help out. John A. Macdonald, over a dozen large whiskeys with his mates, declared, "The Métis government wash (hic) illegal. But I'll grant Riel and the Métis amneshtee (urp). Is it your shout, Nigel?" Four hundred British and 800 Canadian troops (a large portion of the army) left for Red River to deliver this valentine. No sooner had they clanked out of sight than the Fenians attacked Quebec. As usual, the attack failed and the Fenians retreated to the George Washington Tavern across the border to drown their sorrows.

By the time the expeditionary force arrived, the Métis, who had been warned of their arrival, had decamped. Not surprisingly, they sensed trouble coming. (It was difficult to ignore the noise and dust made by 1,200 soldiers and accompanying wagons loaded down with officer's liquor cabinets and dining sets.) The Canadian soldiers were especially ticked off, as it had been a lousy three-month journey, most of it on foot and they had been promised a hanging. Manitoba joined Confederation in 1870.

81

Farther west, B.C. joined the confederation in 1871, after being promised a connection to the rest of Canada. B.C. might have settled for a footpath, but John A. had visions of powerful steam locomotives thundering through mountain passes and pulling strings of well-stocked club cars, with himself passed out in one of them. B.C. got a railroad.

Kaiser Wilhelm I finally settled the long-simmering dispute between the US and Canada over the location of the border through the Gulf and San Juan Islands. Although the Americans had invaded the San Juans some years earlier, the Brits had done nothing to throw them out, so the Kaiser just let everyone stay where they were. B.C. also got its second premier, Amor De Cosmos – the first of a long line of wackos and Fruitloops to lead the province.

To keep peace out west, the Feds created The North West Mounted Police: they were forerunners to the RCMP, and their mandate included upholding law and order and strengthening federal influence over the new territories. The Mounties also existed to cut off the supply of US whiskey flowing across the border. It wasn't so much that the natives were dying of alcohol poisoning: the real crime was that smuggled US whiskey wasn't taxed.

The NWMP were also to make sure the natives were kept in their place and bully those who hadn't signed treaties. The Cree were the last holdouts. Because of their petulance they were denied government rations, essential to their survival since traditional sources of food had been hunted to extinction by white settlers. Finally, in 1882, dying of starvation and disease, the Cree gave in and signed treaty No. Six, which was just as lousy as treaties 1, 2, 3, 4 and 5.

If there were any popularity polls in 1873, they would have shown John A. riding high. That was, until news broke that he and members of his Conservative government had received thousands of dollars in

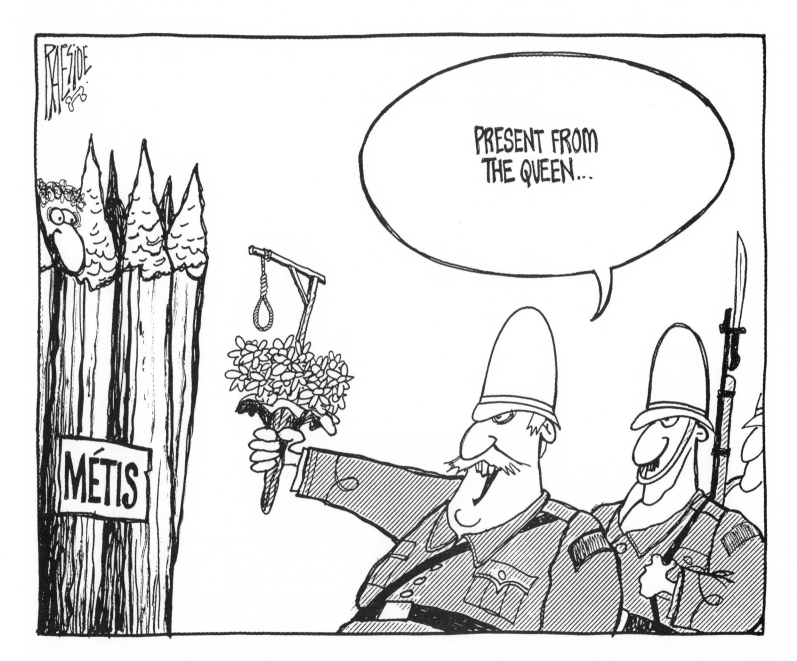

83

non-repayable campaign loans from the American-backed Canadian Pacific Railroad Company. The railroad was about to be awarded the contract to build a transcontinental railroad, along with the millions of acres of land and mineral rights that went along with it. John A. tried to weasel his way out the scandal, but the government fell, defeated mainly by party members miffed they weren't included in the payoff. Five years later all was forgotten, with voters returning John A. and his Tories to power.

With the railroad, came the essentials; tons of booze, a whole new batch of diseases and the first Eaton's catalogue. The Feds were pouring money into the CPR millions at a time. Every few miles of track brought new moans from CPR directors complaining they were broke. No one knew where the money went. It sure didn't go into the Chinese navvies' pockets, as they were paid slave wages and treated worse than dogs. Some of the money to pay for the railroad was raised by charging a head tax on Oriental immigrants, with another tax imposed when they left for home, usually in the form of a pathetic pile of ashes in an urn. The Chinese immigrants were more than welcome when there was lots of nasty low-paid work to go around, but when construction of the CPR was finished, and white Canadians were competing for jobs against the traditionally lower-paid Chinese, things turned ugly. Chinese immigrants were mugged, had their boats sunk,

their businesses looted and their homes trashed. The B.C. government introduced legislation which raised the head tax and made it mandatory for Chinese immigrants to fill out lengthy and complicated immigration forms – in English.

Louis Riel and the Métis, who were still operating in Saskatchewan and Manitoba, teamed up with the disgruntled Cree and Stoney tribes to make a last stand against the Canadian and British Militia. The Métis and native fighters didn't stand a chance. Coming so soon after the Battle of Little Big Horn, public sentiment had turned against the Plains Indians and Canadians were as keen as the army to finish off these troublemakers so they could get on with the job of turning the Prairies into an English country garden. Riel was finally caught and sentenced to death for treason – by a jury of white settlers. After the sentencing, there was a huge groundswell of opinion that Riel should be pardoned, or at least have his death sentence commuted. John A. was determined to make an example of him, even though there were hardly any Métis left to be inspired. Riel and eight others were hanged in Regina in November 1885.

After 4,670 kilometres of track, millions of dollars and dozens of lives lost, the first CPR train rolled into Port Moody on the West Coast, June 6, 1886. Exactly five years later to the day, John A. Macdonald died. It is hoped that Louis Riel met him at the Pearly Gates with a baseball bat.

Life in the Canadian west wasn't as romantic as the lurid promotional posters circulating Europe led prospective immigrants to believe. Many families stepped off a train in the middle of nowhere, in the middle of winter, with only a few dollars in their pockets. Those who weren't snuffed out by the cold had tough sledding ahead, barely scratching a living out of nothing. Lonely bachelors resorted to mail-order brides. Those early dating services did a booming business, enticing young women over from Europe with offers of a new life and ruggedly handsome men. The new life was usually worse than the domestic drudgery they had left behind and the handsome men were often hard-drinking, narrow-minded, battle-scarred wife beaters.

The Yukon goldrush of 1898 was a shot in the arm for free enterprisers, many of whom had also operated in the California and B.C. gold rushes. The Yukon suddenly found itself bulging at the seams with miners, merchants, thieves and prostitutes – similar to the assortment on Parliament Hill today. The saloons were doing a roaring trade, relieving miners of their gold as fast as they could dig it up. The only busier establishment was the NWMP lockup. Prosperity out west meant that the east, which controlled government, banks and businesses, was going through a boom of its own. Architects competed with each other to see who could design the most outrageous Victorian mansions: Before long, massive monuments to excess began sprouting up all over the country.

To celebrate the turn of the century, England got itself involved in another war, this time in South Africa. It wasn't long before appeals went out in Canada for soldiers to help defend the Empire from the dreaded Boers. After mulling over the request for a minute or two, the Canadian government sent over men, horses and supplies to bale out the British. Meanwhile, stone masons prepared blocks of marble for the memorials to the war dead that would soon be appearing in town

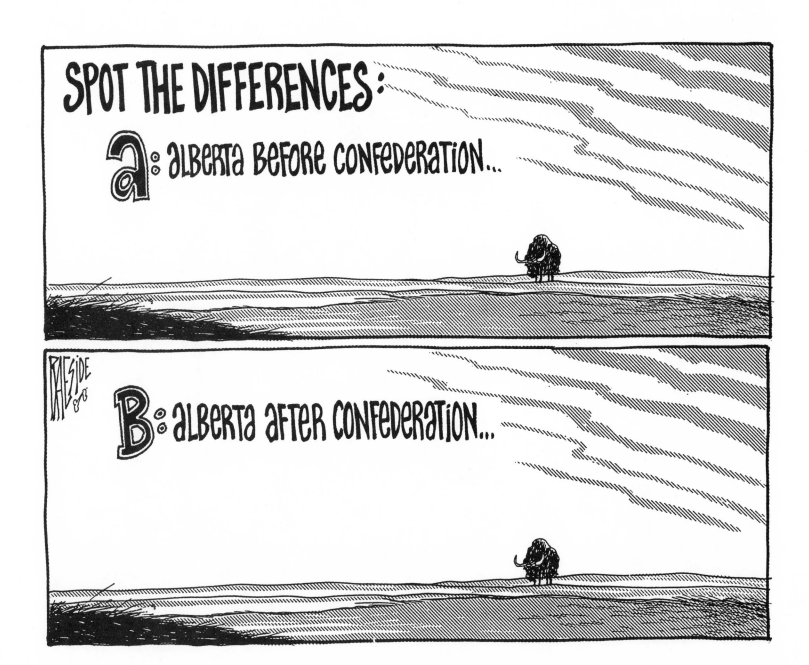

SPOT THE DIFFERENCES:

a: ALBERTA BEFORE CONFEDERATION...

B: ALBERTA AFTER CONFEDERATION...

squares all over Canada. This proved a fitting beginning to a century
in which wars would claim thousands of Canadian lives.

Alberta became a member of the confederation in 1905.

Farther east, although manufacturing had been flourishing in Montreal for some time in the form of textile mills, heavy industry didn't
make its debut until 1908, when the McLaughlin Motor Car Company
of Oshawa, Ontario, made a deal with the Buick Motor Company to
purchase Buick engines for cars produced in Canada. This opened up a
whole new chapter in Canadian travel lore: traffic accidents, drunk
driving, dating and drive-ins.

While many immigrants were suffering in urban slum conditions
not much better than those described by Charles Dickens, the Laurier
Liberals spent a few million dollars buying the clapped-out ex-Royal
navy battleship, Niobe. Nobody was sure what her role would be, other
than as a terrific place to hold official receptions. Laurier also entered
into discussions with the Americans over a free trade deal between the
US and Canada. (It wasn't until 79 years later that Canada and the US
hammered out a free trade deal – the US got the deal and Canada got
hammered.) Laurier was confident he had the support of the Canadian
people, a confidence that disappeared in September 1911, after the Liberals were thrashed by the anti free trade forces led by Robert Borden's
Tories. One of Borden's first acts was to grant boundary extensions to
Quebec, Ontario and Manitoba. This wasn't likely to affect the native
population, as there weren't too many left anyway.

THERE GOES THE NEIGHBOURHOOD

Under the thin veneer of gentility that Canada liked to project to the world, lay the life of the average working stiff. Canada was still a frontier land and life was cheap. As industry became more efficient, labourers were no longer in such demand. Many unemployed Canadians resented the fact that many of the Chinese and Japanese were still employed, although making much less money than their Caucasian counterparts.

While European leaders were loading ammunition trucks and laying out the body bags in preparation for WW I, Canadian officials were grappling with what to do over the *Komagata Maru* anchored in Vancouver harbour, and packed with Sikh immigrants requesting permission to come ashore. Since the government had a policy of restricting non-white immigration, the immigrants remained trapped on the ship for two months without much food or water. The ship was eventually forced out of Canadian waters at gunpoint. The incident was soon forgotten as Britain declared war on Germany. As we were still part of the Empire, Canada was at war too.

Thanks to a great PR campaign and advances in transportation, Canada was starting to fill up with new immigrants, many of whom didn't speak the language, and brought with them alien customs. (All very shocking to the original settlers, but very familiar to the natives.)

Chapter 5

THE INSANE YEARS

At the time it sounded like a pretty noble cause: join the army, sail over to Europe, stroll into Berlin and teach the Hun the meaning of respect over tea and cakes. Besides, "it would all be over by Christmas." One can only hope the cretin who dreamed up that phrase ended up in the trenches four years later. None of the farm boys who rushed to sign up had the slightest inkling just how badly managed the war would be and how many thousands of lives would be lost just to capture a few feet of fly-blown mud. Canadian generals who were eager to add to their medal collections and make names for themselves, rushed the new recruits through only the most basic training involving, at the most, wandering about a parade ground with a sack full of rocks on their backs, then banging off their rifles in the general direction of a paper silhouette of the Kaiser.

Soon, the troops were packed into overloaded trains and bullied onto flotillas of ships that in peacetime would have been scrapped. Arriving in France, sicker than dogs but anxious to get the job done, they squelched off into the pools of mud that made up the front line. Their high-ranking officers, meanwhile, were often forced to make do with requisitioned French chateaux with barely enough room for a few comfy armchairs and a well-stocked drinks trolley.

Canadian manufacturers at home were hoping it *wouldn't* be over by Christmas. Showered with government money, they were churning out often shoddy equipment for the troops, from boots that fell apart after a few weeks, to the infamous Canadian-made Ross Rifle. The Ross proved totally useless in a battlefield situation, prompting many Canadian soldiers to risk their lives sneaking out into no man's land to relieve dead English soldiers of their coveted Lee Enfield rifles.

It wasn't until 1916 that Sam Hughes, the minister for the Canadian militia finally gave up defending the Ross Rifle and switched

over to the more reliable Enfield. No one knows how many lives were lost through failed and lousy equipment, as there were rarely many survivors of these battles and those who did survive wanted only to go home and forget what had happened. To be fair, it wasn't just greedy manufacturers who were responsible for the rows of white crosses: tactical and battlefield decisions were often absurd to the point of lunacy. Ypres, Vimy Ridge, The Somme, Hill 70, Passchendaele – all these names became part of Canadian history only because of boneheaded German and English generals anxious to move their drinks trolleys a few inches closer to Paris or Berlin.

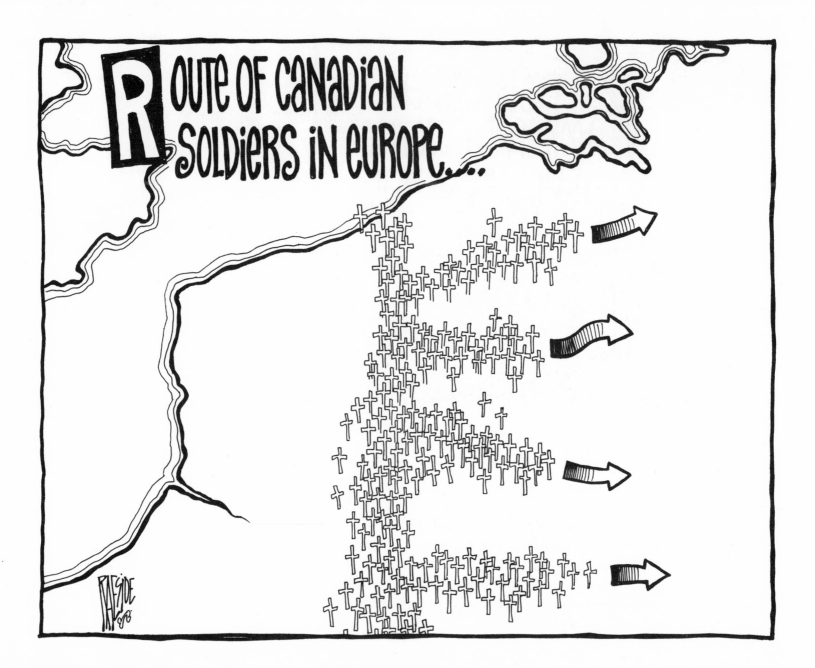

As the soldiers sank deeper into the mud, costs to keep them there were rising. Ottawa finally took the opportunity to introduce the long-threatened income tax along with conscription. Now, not only could you be forced to spend a winter rotting in the trenches, but your parents would have the privilege of paying for the artillery shell that landed beside you by mistake and blew your head off.

However, you didn't have to go to France to have your head blown off. If you were sitting in O'Grady's Halifax Beer Emporium on December 6, 1917, there wouldn't be much left of you. A munitions ship blew up in the harbour, levelling much of the city.

In the midst of the confusing war years, there were two new developments. First, Quebec legislators floated the idea of separation. They were no doubt anxious to distance themselves from a war that appeared to be dragging on until the last soldier defending Britain disappeared into the mud. Second, Ottawa, recognizing there were some problems with rights in confederation, gave women the vote. To the relief of the male politicians, so many strings were attached that the chances were very slim of the average Canadian woman voting in anything more than the race for county dogcatcher.

On November 11, 1918, World War I ended the way most wars end, with both sides proclaiming victory and the generals retiring to their clubs to lie about the number of enemy they personally killed. The soldiers were dragged out of the mud, hosed off and stuffed into the same leaking ships they came over on. Once ashore, they were told to go home and forget about everything. They returned to a country alarmingly short of young men to work in industry and on the farms. Canada had also changed physically during the war. Most of the accessible trees had been whacked down during the war. Logging railways were now sneaking into the wilderness, bringing with them more efficient ways to denude the forests.

Following the end of the war, what started as a small strike by Winnipeg steelworkers grew into an all-out general strike. By the time it was over, two strikers were dead, and dozens injured or sitting in prison cells. Now that the war was over, the government went back to Europe to solicit more immigrants to Canada to fill the spaces left by the war. This time the government was hoping for well-off English gentleman farmers with a history of voting Tory, unlike the previous policy of accepting anybody who had a heartbeat and could pick up a shovel.

Canada got a change of clowns in 1921, with a minority government led by William Lyon Mackenzie King, best known for discussing affairs of state with his dog Pat, who was a spiritual medium for King's dead mother. He didn't do such a bad job of running the show, so some suggested the dog become Minister of External Affairs.

One of King's first accomplishments was to travel to England to push for Canadian autonomy as a reward for sending over half its male population to be used up by British military planners. To King's credit, he was the first Canadian PM to turn down a request from Britain for troops to help bail it out of yet another mess, the tiff with Turkey made famous by T.E. Lawrence.

A couple of years later, Canada, in a daring move, put the old Union Jack in the closet and officially flew the new red ensign, a mishmash of crests, leaves and crowns totally unreadable from a distance of more than ten feet. The most visible component was the Union Jack in the corner. None of that mattered; the important thing was that it was ours.

One more benefit from the war was the increased use of the airplane in Canada's north: great for surveying and mapping; terrific for spotting seal herds on ice floes.

All this time, the Group of Seven, as the painters came to be known, were faithfully recording on canvas the soon-to-vanish Canadian wilderness, oblivious to the fact that, years later, art dealers would make fortunes from paintings the artists would have been lucky to sell for a square meal.

One aspect of Canadian society the Group of Seven never depicted was the Roaring Twenties. (More like the Whimpering Twenties, compared to what our cousins south of the border were getting up to.) But, in the spirit of the times, Canada went out and got pissed for five years. Hemlines were climbing up legs and inhibitions were dropping faster than Mackenzie King's re-election chances.

In a departure from tradition, Canadians were now running liquor across to the US which had been dry for some time now. Canadian booze was pouring across the border in the same volume as water over Niagara Falls. Canadian authorities turned a blind eye to it; as long as the taxes on the liquor were paid, it was none of their business where it went.

In 1926, Mackenzie King's Liberals went down to defeat. The Tories, under Arthur Meighen, lasted three days before their defeat

111

under a non-confidence vote. Two months later, King, his dog and his dead mum were back in the prime minister's office. Shades of *Psycho*. . . .

Everything was looking up for Canada: rail services were expanding; more people were buying cars and getting killed in them; immigrant farmers were starting to see modest profits from their dirt patches – then the Wall Street stock market collapsed, taking everyone with it.

The lines of unemployed started in the east and moved quickly west. By the time the full impact hit the west, a severe drought had set in, turning once lush farms into sand dunes. The banks didn't help much by foreclosing at a steady clip. This was necessary, they said, to protect the banks themselves from bankruptcy. It worked – hardly any Canadian banks went under during the Depression, while thousands of Canadian businesses died.

Although the whole country was suffering from unemployment, the Prairies were hit the hardest. Most of Saskatchewan dried up and blew into Alberta. Canadian banks took the opportunity to get involved, turfing families off their farms and auctioning off what remained to the highest bidder. Some farmers in better financial shape were able to amass huge tracts of land from these "auctions."

Local governments introduced a system of relief payments of $1
to $2 a day for those who picked up shovels and participated in make-
work projects. Clearly this was a pittance, but better than nothing
(which was exactly what most men west of Ontario had in 1930.)

The Depression helped bring about the demise of King's Liberals.
In their place rose the Tories, led by R.B. Bennett. Two months into his
mandate Bennett must have considered giving it all back to King: the
Communist party was having a field day organizing groups of unemployed into armed mobs; fights were breaking out in cities all across the
country and the few remaining prairie farms that hadn't been repos-
sessed by the banks had shrivelled up and blown away. Farmers would
load their families and anything else they could carry onto their vehi-
cles and wheeze through the dust storms to the nearest city to look
for work. These overloaded old heaps soon took on the nickname,

"Bennett Buggies." True to Canadian political tradition, their namesake refused to change previous policy, ignoring suggestions to institute a "dole" system instead of the nationwide government make-work projects. For pennies a day, the unemployed would dig a hole on a Monday, fill it in on Tuesday and dig it up again on Wednesday. All smashing good exercise for a malnourished office clerk who had never held anything bigger than a pen in his hands before.

One bright spot at that time was the discovery, in 1933, of a few human bones in the high Arctic, thought to belong to the Franklin

Expedition. As no Inuit knives and forks were found nearby, the conclusion was that, whoever they were, they'd died of natural causes.

While Canadians were being starved by the Depression, choked by dust and beaten by riot policemen, Europeans were waking up to a brand new nightmare. The Nazi party had left the beer halls and was roaming the halls of the German Reichstag – until they burned it down. Hitler and his psychopathic cronies were embarking on their program to exterminate anyone who didn't have blond hair, blue eyes and syphilis. Stories were beginning to leak out about Nazi atrocities, but they were so incredible few believed them. Meanwhile, anti-semitism was also thriving in Canada.

As an antidote to the world's lunacy, Canadians went berserk over the birth of the Dionne quintuplets, in 1934. The government set up a special nursery, supposedly to keep the girls isolated from fatal diseases. But this only isolated them from their parents and targeted them for the shameful exploitation that followed. You'd have been hard pressed in those days to pick up a cup, placemat, record, newspaper, apron or baby shoe that didn't have the Dionnes staring sadly back at you.

The reality of the Depression in the west hit the Feds when relief camp workers, fed up with conditions, began to march on Ottawa. Their numbers swelling, they commandeered a train and rolled as far as Regina before the police moved in under orders from the government. When the shooting, clubbing and gassing were over, one policeman was dead and dozens of marchers injured. Bennett's mismanagement

119

paved the way for King's return to power on October 14, 1935, in a one-sided rout similar to the one in Regina a few months earlier. In 1938, King freed up $125 million for relief payments and public works projects. But for the thousands living in tents and under bridges, it was just a case of too little too late.

By the time that King Edward ran off with American divorcée Wally Simpson, leaving behind an outraged family and a titillated public, the Nazis were helping out a fellow despot, Generalissimo Franco. The world "tut tutted" as the Fascists, assisted by those anxious to please the Nazis, bombed and strafed their way across Spain. An international brigade was formed to help fight the Fascists. Canadian Communists formed the Mackenzie – Papineau brigade and sailed over to be chewed up by Luftwaffe divebombers.

Just as it had in 1931, when the Japanese shot and raped their way across Manchuria, the world "tch tchd" as Italy's Mussolini was machine-gunning defenceless Abyssinian tribesmen and the Soviet Union's Joe Stalin was doing a little housecleaning, killing millions of his own people every time his toothache acted up.

Meanwhile, back on the reservations, natives were dropping like flies as a TB epidemic finished off whoever had survived the previous cholera epidemic. On the West Coast, another wave of discrimination was washing against Oriental immigrants. On the East Coast, a boatload of Jewish refugees from Germany was turned away at gunpoint by the Canadian government after being denied entrance to Cuba, the US, Argentina, Panama, and Uruguay. The boat eventually sailed back to the concentration camps in Germany. Three months later, Canada was at war with Germany.

Manufacturers in Canada who had been suffering through the last few years of the Depression, couldn't believe their luck – another war. Office strongrooms all across the country were being cleaned out in preparation for the sacks of money that would soon be coming their way if this war was as lucrative as the last one. Canadians were flocking to the banks buying War Bonds, Victory Bonds, Strangle-a-Hun Bonds. . . . There was something comforting about fighting the Bosche again; we'd been doing it for years and besides, it would all be over by Christmas. One bright spot for the average Canadian working stiff: the war meant lots of jobs – as long as you didn't mind pounding rivets into the side of a warship.

The first Canadian casualties were, as usual, civilians. On September 3, 1939, the SS *Athenia*, packed with North Americans putting distance between themselves and Hitler, ran into a German torpedo off the Hebrides, losing 90 of its passengers overboard. Adding to the war dead two months later, was Dr. Norman Bethune, a Canadian who had left Montreal to fight Fascism. Bethune died of blood poisoning in China, where he had been treating Chinese casualties during the Japanese occupation of Manchuria. It seemed the Manchurian war had gone from "something really should be done" to "who gives a damn" on the world's list of priorities.

While the Nazis were herding Polish Jews into the Warsaw Ghetto, Mackenzie King was re-elected prime minister – yet again. King temporarily kept his pre-election promise and refused to introduce conscription (mainly to keep Quebecers happy.) The government also used the war as an excuse to ban the Communist party and outlaw the pacifist Jehovah's Witness religion. Shipments of wartime materials to Britain increased, and in exchange, Canada received shiploads of British children, evacuated from cities that Hitler was about to reduce to rubble.

On July 11, 1940, the Feds finally announced the introduction of the Unemployment Insurance Act, the salvation for those who were "between jobs." As most Canadian men were now employed either building guns or shooting them, no one paid much attention. The Canada–US defence pact was also signed at the same time and in the spirit of all deals signed with the Yanks, it gave the American arms manufacturers freer access to Canadian requisition officers and access to Canadian territory and bases should the "need" arise. . . . Canada got nothing.

The Liberals began sneaking conscription through Parliament in October 1940. They began by requiring all single men between 21 and 24 to report for 30 days of basic training. This prompted a rush on jewellery stores and marriage bureaus. By volunteering to work in labour camps, a few were able to avoid 30 days of being shouted at while wearing a uniform two sizes too small. Shortly after, the training period was upped to four months and Canadian women, who up to now had been doing their part organizing knitting bees and churning out thousands of shapeless, gaily coloured socks for the fashion-conscious soldiers overseas, were now eligible for war duty at home.

The conscription issue was a *pomme chaud* in Quebec. Mackenzie King had deliberately gone against his election vow for no conscription; he asked the nation to release him from his promise. In the resulting plebiscite, English-speaking Canadians voted overwhelmingly for conscription, while French Canadians said *'non'* at a rate of 9 to 1. Conscription was enforced. (Mac's dog must have received mixed signals from Ma King that day.)

The British, meanwhile, had been pressuring Canadians to get involved in a heroic, futile gesture to stop the Japanese army which was sweeping across Asia at 50 mph. The Japanese bombing of Pearl Harbour was the excuse needed to send 1,975 more Canadian troops to Hong Kong, to defend the colony that had been under siege by the Japanese since December 8. The soldiers landed in Hong Kong minus adequate training and most of their equipment. A few days later, what was left of the force were being starved and beaten in Japanese prison camps. Concerned that Japanese and Japanese-Canadians on the West Coast were spies, the Feds began rounding up all Japanese-Canadians and Japanese nationals in Canada, seizing their assets and locking them up in prison camps. Some Canadian officials, involved in the disposal of Japanese assets in Canada became very wealthy from sweetheart land deals. Most of the Japanese-Canadian property was never returned after the war.

The war was getting closer to home. In June, a Japanese sub took a few pot shots at a lighthouse off Victoria. The only casualties were two broken windows, a cracked teacup and the lighthouse keeper's cat, Bob, who wouldn't come out from under the bed for three days. Casualties were a little heavier at the Allied invasion of Dieppe two months later.

Supposedly launched to test invasion techniques, the Allied effort rapidly became an example of how *not* to invade a coastline defended by thousands of Nazis, armed to the teeth and hiding behind reinforced

129

concrete bunkers. Most of the guinea pigs were Canadian. As in the invasion of Gallipoli 27 years earlier, the troops were commanded by British generals tucked away in a warship far removed from the battle and from reality. Soldiers were mown down by the hundreds as soon as they were pushed off the landing craft. Most never even made it up the beach. To the Germans, it was like a shooting gallery at an amusement park. When the slaughter was over, the Allies lost 993 and 1,874 were taken prisoner. German casualties were comparatively light, including a bratwurst and sauerkraut sandwich bruised by a stray bullet.

Britain was now being supplied by convoys of merchant ships protected by Canadian warships. All were being torpedoed on a regular basis by packs of German U-boats lurking in the North Atlantic. In the factories there were still plenty of men working at jobs classified by the government as "essential" and the unions were still active despite the war. Strikes were becoming common. Wages were the main issue, with demands for a closed shop next on the list. The Feds suspected that the dreaded CCF were behind most of the strikes. Formed in 1933, the Co-operative Commonwealth Federation became Canada's first socialist party and vigorously opposed the Tories, who assumed that poverty itself was a crime.

On July 10, 1943 something finally went right for Canadian troops overseas. The Allies landed in Sicily and battled their way across the island, eventually landing at Salerno on the mainland. At the same time, Mussolini formally retired from the Axis alliance mainly because he was hung upside down by the Italian resistance. The Italian army collapsed; the Germans, who had become used to the agreeable Italian climate, decided to stay on.

June 6, 1944: D-Day. The Allies invaded France via Normandy, with the Canadian division landing on Juno Beach. This time the invasion was planned months ahead of time and was meant to succeed.

Dodging minefields and German bullets, the Canadian battalion got further inland by nightfall than the American or British forces who landed on beaches nearby. As the Canadians advanced further, German resistance stiffened and the casualties mounted.

At home, the CCF formed the next provincial government in Saskatchewan and construction on the Chalk River atomic energy plant was started, part of the American-sponsored Manhattan project to develop an atomic bomb which was still just a gleam in a madman's eye.

Mackenzie King played host to Churchill and Roosevelt in Quebec City in September 1944. King had become little more than the tea lady at these meetings, but, fortunately for Canadian soldiers hiding in trenches around Europe, at least the Canadian government retained the final say as to where they would be deployed. Otherwise, there might have been dozens of Dieppes. In December 1944, Parliament finally approved an overseas draft. Quebec MPs were incensed and accused the CCF and the Liberals of collusion.

The whole squalid mess was over in Europe on May 7, 1945. To celebrate VE day, hundreds of sailors in Halifax went on the rampage, attempting to leave the city in the same condition that most European cities were in after Adolf and his mates were finished with them.

Now all that was left was to finish off Japan. Judging by the fanaticism with which the Japanese defended tiny bits of coral, no one was looking forward to invading the country. We were saved that bother after Hiroshima and Nagasaki disappeared under an atomic cloud. Japan tossed in their headbands.

Having made it through two world wars, it was time for Canada to take stock; although we were down a few thousand young men, we now had the freedom to go it alone as a nation. It was nice not to have to ask permission before polluting a lake, clearcutting a forest or poisoning the air.

Chapter 6

PICKING THROUGH THE LEFTOVERS

With the Japanese military roaming the streets of Tokyo in rags, looking for scraps, attention could be turned to the thousands of Japanese-Canadians interned in Canada. After four years of being treated worse than cattle, many were told they would now be deported. The fact that millions of lives had just been lost defending the rights of persecuted minorities was lost on Canadians, who celebrated the end of the war with 'Hate-an-Oriental' month. The fighting had stopped, but the madness continued.

Along with returning soldiers came shiploads of warbrides, many accompanied by babies. It appeared that Canadian servicemen had been doing more than banging off their guns at Jerry. It was a shock to these women, coming from a country that was starved from six years of rationing and crippled by war debts, to step off the boat and wade through nylons, perfume and clothes that fit. (Culture shock and loneliness soon followed the euphoria.)

Returning veterans weren't looking for nylons and perfume. They needed jobs. Thousands of soldiers were going back to civilian life to try and pick up where they left off. In many cases their previous lives, jobs and girlfriends were gone. Job prospects didn't improve much as

another wave of immigrants arrived in Canada. Displaced People – D.P.s – arrived from Europe by the thousands, anxious to take the veterans' places cutting down trees and digging up the land.

Like a three-year-old being given the keys to a stately home without parental supervision, Canada was granted the power to amend the British North America Act on its own, without having to ask permission from the British Crown. This set in motion years of endless debates, committees and hearings that have since bored Canadians and bank-rupted the country. At that time, no one could agree on how to go about actually amending the old BNA act, so a parliamentary committee was struck to study the problem and it was conveniently forgotten for the time being.

In a seemingly unrelated development, a new magazine published out of Montreal, *Cité Libre*, appeared in the nicotine-stained fingers of reformers in Quebec. Published by Gérard Pelletier and Pierre Elliott Trudeau, it went largely unnoticed by the rest of the country (and in Quebec, itself) but it did help make a name for Trudeau. The Jesuit-trained son of a wealthy gas station owner, Trudeau was gathering some attention in Quebec. The provincial scene was dominated by Conservative Maurice Duplessis, who had been running Quebec as a profitable family business and he didn't take kindly to interference from reactionaries like Trudeau.

Canada was by now quite independent from Britain and it was comforting for parents of military-age children to know they were no longer required to send Junior over to be mown down in the English war *du jour*. We were instead part of the United Nations, a forum created to prevent a repeat of the last 2,000 years of blood-letting. The UN was also a good hiding place for ex-Nazis who had something to offer to the West (such as rocket plans). The UN worked wonderfully until December 1950, when Canadian soldiers packed their toothbrushes and sailed over to South Korea, which had been invaded a

few months earlier by its Marxist brothers from the North. The North Koreans had the invaluable assistance of the Chinese who saw the scrap as a perfect opportunity to spread the good word about the advantages of having your toenails pulled out by those in a Communist government.

Military planners had been busy perfecting weapons developed during World War II and were keen to try them out on real people. With superior firepower and God (naturally) on our side, no one expected the fight to last more than a few months. As usual, the military planners weren't earning their salaries. Winter set in and the UN troops found themselves staring across frozen mud at thousands of well-armed Chinese with bad attitudes. Another quick expedition to liberate a country from the forces of evil had degenerated into a stalemate over a few featureless hills with interesting names like "107" or "60." The Canadians did a sterling job of defending Korea, despite often facing the enemy without the benefit of supporting South Korean troops who frequently disappeared as soon as the North Koreans stuck their noses over their trenches.

Meanwhile, Princess Elizabeth became Queen in February 1952, after the death of her father, King George VI. Since her coronation, Liz, Phil and the corgis have made numerous forays to the old family estate. Each trip would see Liz stuffed into the back of a car wielding her patented karate-chop wave at her (once) loyal subjects.

Also coming to power that year was British Columbia's W.A.C. Bennett and his Social Credit party, made up of the usual load of shysters that western Canadian politics seems to attract. W.A.C. dominated B.C. politics for the next 25 years, eventually passing over leadership of the party, like a family heirloom, to his son Bill.

In 1953, the Liberals, under Louis St. Laurent, anxious to assert Canadian sovereignty in previously unoccupied Arctic areas, forcibly relocated Inuit natives from their traditional southern Arctic hunting

grounds to barren unoccupied territory further north. No one thought of checking first to see if there was anything to eat in the new territory. There wasn't. Many of the Inuit starved to death.

At the same time that our Arctic sovereignty was being guarded by an emaciated collection of Inuit forced to eat their clothes for food, Ottawa was giving the Americans control over vital areas of Canada with the joint building of the St. Lawrence Seaway and construction of the Northern DEW Line, built to detect Soviet missiles that never came.

A federal election was held in 1957 and the Tories, under John Diefenbaker, were flaying the Liberals alive over fiscal mismanagement,

unemployment, the proposed Trans–Canada Pipeline and close ties with the USA. The Tories barely clawed their way in to form a minority government, relying on backroom deals with the CCF and Social Credit to keep them in power. It wasn't until the next election a year later that Diefenbaker was able to form a majority government. Dief immediately signed a new Canada–US defence pact and went on a shopping trip for a few nuclear missiles.

Ostensibly to switch Canada's air defences from jet fighters to missiles, Diefenbaker announced in 1959 that he was scrapping the Avro Arrow, the only 100% Canadian-built jet fighter, putting 14,000 Canadians out of work, but lessening the competition for US aircraft manufacturers. The five Arrows that had already been built were ordered cut into pieces and scrapped.

Canada got a brand new political party in 1961, with the launch of the New Democratic Party, led by Tommy Douglas. Promising more social programs and a higher standard of living, Douglas inspired many young Canadians, who normally would have nothing to do with the out-of-touch-with-reality Liberal or Tory parties, to get involved in politics. (He also attracted a large contingent of hairy people in bad corduroy jackets.) The same year, the NDP government in Saskatchewan introduced Canada's first medical plan, giving Saskatchewan residents free health care. It wasn't until July 1, 1968 that the whole country got medicare plans based on the Saskatchewan system.

Nationalism was growing in Quebec and a small group of hardliners was calling for secession. No one paid too much attention until an obscure fringe group, the *Front de Liberation du Quebec* (FLQ to their *amis*) started blowing up mailboxes in Westmount, the mostly English-speaking section of Montreal. Nothing much was accomplished, but Canada Post had a terrific excuse why mail wasn't being delivered on time.

A few wrecked mailboxes were nothing compared to what would happen if any of the nuclear warheads the Tories were considering buying accidentally detonated on Canadian soil. The debate raged as to whether Canada should participate in the arms race, or rely on US nuclear protection. Either way, Canada could become a radioactive wasteland if anything nasty happened.

This wasn't helping the Tories in the polls. On April 8, 1963 the Liberals formed a minority government. Led by Lester B. Pearson, the Liberals then lurched through two elections. Pearson was the prime minister responsible for setting up the first of endless Royal Commissions on bilingualism and biculturalism. Like all the commissions since, it was savaged by the opposition, and ignored by Canadians. Pearson and W.A.C. Bennett also masterminded the giveaway of Canadian hydro-electric power to the US, carrying on the fine tradition of Ottawa rolling over with her feet in the air as soon as anyone wearing red, white and blue appeared.

an external affairs guide to dealing with the United States on....

On November 22, 1963, John F. Kennedy was assassinated. Kennedy's corpse wasn't even cold before the US plunged even further into the jungles of Vietnam. Canada's official role in the war was as a refuge for the thousands of young American draftees who crossed the border to escape a war that was only marginally more insane than most previous conflicts.

Meanwhile, Paul Hellyer, the Liberal defence minister, introduced a white paper (isn't most paper white?) on integrating the Canadian armed forces. Causing near apoplexy in the mess halls, the plan was

The New, Unified Armed Forces Uniform...

Reinforced hat for protection against falling parts.

Puke-green uniform colour to hide annoying rust stains.

Handy multi-purpose tool kit for the numerous running repairs.

Asbestos pants-protection against burst steam pipes.

Reinforced knees for when begging for more govt. funding.

Sturdy shoes for hiking through miles of red tape.

eventually brought in, merging the army, navy and airforce into one drab olive-green uniform. Parking commissionaires looked smarter.

Not satisfied with just gutting the armed forces, the Liberals started hinting seriously about repatriating the BNA Act to Canada, and setting up a constitutional amending formula. And while they were at it, why not change the flag? Although the old flag would never have won any beauty-in-design competitions, the new one did not include the Union Jack, which outraged monarchists. Despite opposition from across the country (especially Victoria) the new maple leaf flag was hauled up the Peace Tower flag pole on February 15, 1965.

The Commons finally approved a universal Canadian pension plan, supported by employees and employers. Under the CPP, a retired person could expect the princely sum of $75.00 per month. Taking into account inflation, the amount hasn't changed much in 25 years. . . .

Canadians were on the whole unaware of the nation's flora and fauna until the seal hunt in Newfoundland became public. For decades, local sealers took to the ice each March, killing thousands of pups who lay helpless on the floes. Armed with clubs and knives, the sealers clubbed the animals senseless, then skinned off their white pelts, often while the seal was still alive. The federal fisheries minister

was deluged with letters from outraged Canadians demanding an end to the slaughter. As a compromise, sealers grudgingly accepted new regulations that required them to kill the seal before skinning it. It wasn't until 20 years later that the threat of an international boycott of Canadian fish products finally put an end to the seal hunt.

It wasn't just the bloodstained ice that was catching the attention of the public. Plumes of toxic emissions from heavy industry in places like Hamilton were no longer just signs of a healthy economy. Fish with cancerous growths on them were being caught and birds' eggs were

sterile. In 1969, a group of environmentalists chartered a fishing boat and sailed up to Amchitka Island off Alaska to protest against US nuclear testing there. This was the beginning of the Greenpeace organization.

Ottawa, under pressure from social groups and the Ministry of Native Affairs, finally relented and released a few dollars for improvements to Indian reservations. As late as 1970, few native homes had even the most basic facilities such as running water or septic tanks.

The only natives the average Canadian came into contact with were those who dressed up in ceremonial costumes and performed at

fairs or exhibitions. Expo '67 in Montreal showcased the usual group of tarted-up natives performing for the amusement of tourists who hadn't been within a hundred miles of a reservation, or ever seen the effects of polio and poverty on its inhabitants. Those who did point out the deplorable state the natives lived in were usually dismissed with, "They like it that way" or, "What did they do with all the money we gave them?" and of course, the classic, "Who cares? They're all pissed anyway."

Expo '67 and Canada's centennial made for one heck of a party for the white people: fireworks on Parliament Hill; centennial centres; fountains built across the country; commemorative coins and stamps; Charles de Gaulle yelling *"Vive le Québec libre"* in Montreal. . . . All great fun, but it had to end sometime. When it did, Canada woke up to a giant hangover in the form of Pierre Trudeau as the new Liberal prime minister, with René Lévesque leading Quebec's nationalist Parti Québécois.

Lévesque was pushing sovereignty association for Quebec, giving the province control over language, culture, government, cigarette sales, parking fines and the like. Trudeau, also a French Canadian, attempted to defuse Quebec nationalism by bringing in the official languages bill, making the entire country bilingual. Manufacturers in

158

English Canada struggled with dimly remembered school French, and dutifully changed their packaging and labels.

None of this did anything to endear the Trudeau government to anglophones in the west, who hinted at their displeasure by never electing a federal Liberal MP west of Manitoba.

In the 1970 Quebec provincial election, the Parti Québécois won seven seats, but were beaten by Robert Bourassa and his Liberals. The FLQ celebrated the victory of a nationalist party by blowing up some more mailboxes.

Six months later, the FLQ ceased to be just a fringe group of crazies; with the kidnapping of British Trade Commissioner James Cross and provincial Liberal Labour Minister Pierre Laporte, they became terrorists. Pierre Trudeau invoked the War Measures Act and the army rolled onto the streets.

James Cross was eventually released unharmed, in exchange for letting two FLQ terrorists fly to Cuba. Pierre Laporte wasn't so lucky; his strangled body was found in the trunk of a car eight days after his abduction. Three of his captors were rounded up and convicted. The two terrorists who had fled to Cuba returned to Canada years later, to receive a full pardon.

Bachelor PM Pierre Trudeau married Margaret Sinclair in a fairytale wedding in Vancouver. The marriage ended eight years later in a fairytale divorce after six years of marriage, a few evenings at Studio 54 and one heck of a night with Mick Jagger and the Rolling Stones.

In the federal election held in November 1972 the NDP won 30 seats and held the balance of power for the Liberals. The Liberals, who would have rather shared power with Typhoid Mary, refused to grovel for NDP support and slithered through the next two years of government, being thrashed from all sides. Finally, after a non-confidence vote in May 1974, the Commons kicked the Liberals out, only to have the electorate kick them back in the July election.

By the mid-70s, fallout from the Yom Kippur war (one of the endless skirmishes between Arabs and Israelis), had put a few holes in Western economies. The Arabs, seething over the West's support for Israel, put aside their internal hatreds just long enough to jack up the price of crude oil by 70%.

This served to shut down western Europe, but gave a wonderful Thanksgiving gift to western Canadian oil producers who had been having a tough time selling Canadian oil which was more expensive to extract and transport. The Liberals put an end to the euphoria by introducing the National Energy Policy, which put a price ceiling on oil pumped for the domestic market, and by creating Petro-Canada, giving the government a seat at the oil producers' table. This did not sit well with the west who saw this as another example of Ottawa interfering with a free market. "Let the Bastards Freeze in the Dark" bumper stickers appeared on pickups across Alberta (in English only).

Further west, in B.C., a four-year experiment with socialism failed. The NDP were slung out and the Socreds returned, under W.A.C. Bennett's son, Bill. Not as outgoing as his father, Bill kept very much to himself and skulked through ten years in power. 1976 was the Year of the Nerd, with the Tories electing Joe Clark as their leader and best hope to defeat the Liberals. Clark beat rival candidate Brian Mulroney, who had spent a fortune on hats and a theme song, only to be defeated by an unknown in a cheap suit.

163

With the invoices still outstanding, Montreal opened the 1976 Olympic Games. Major Jean Drapeau boasted "the Olympics can no more have a deficit than a man can have a baby." (It is rumoured that Dr. Morgentaler, the crusader for women's rights who in 1975 was sent up for 18 months for performing illegal abortions, had visited the mayor's office a number of times.) Immediately after the Games, while the debt was still being counted up, René Lévesque and the Parti Québécois broke into the premier's office, beating Bourassa's Liberals 69–28. French-Canadians were clearly aching for change. Tired of feeling like poor relations, they had not forgotten the ill-treatment of Riel and the Métis on the prairies, nor the furor over the conscription issue. Canada lurched into a new crisis. Lévesque was a hard-line separatist and had repeatedly threatened to take Quebec out of Confederation. For the next few years the country was enthralled, watching Lévesque and Trudeau grappling over the issue of separation. In the heat of negotiations, Trudeau announced that he would resign if Quebec separated. Some Canadians, by now sick and tired of the bickering, were beginning to think that maybe separation could be good for Canada and, at the very least, Trudeau's resignation would do the country a world of good.

Not so enthralled were the national and multinational businesses located in Quebec that had to contend with a series of bizarre laws brought in by the PQ. The Royal Bank and Sun Life were just a couple of the corporations that loaded up their pickups and headed out of town.

It wasn't just the PQ who were eager to translate everything into French; the Feds were busy making air traffic control at some airports bilingual. This was an interesting concept, considering that English is the universal language of air traffic. A number of Canadian pilots went on strike and some foreign carriers refused to take the risk of flying into Canada with one eye on the controls and the other on a French phrase-book.

By 1979, the PQ had announced there would be a referendum on the issue of separation, about the same time that Trudeau announced that he was going ahead with a pet project of his – repatriating the Canadian constitution from England and writing in a few new clauses while he was at it. That was all put on hold June 4, 1979, as the Tories under Joe Clark formed a minority government. John Diefenbaker died of shame two months later. In the confusion, Pierre Trudeau resigned as Liberal leader, but stayed on just long enough to be enticed back when the Tories were surprised by a non-confidence vote nine fumbling months into their mandate. Although the Liberals were returned with a majority on February 18, 1980, only two Liberals were elected west of Ontario.

Quebec voted on sovereignty association May 22, 1980, with 60% voting *non*. Lévesque and the *oui* forces were naturally disappointed. René was clearly a broken and frustrated man; he went from five to ten packs a day, and began wearing ill-fitting, rumpled suits. Despite the

vote, Quebec still went ahead sending out the *oui* storm troopers to enforce the language laws, barring signs in English – businesses continued to flee the province.

Attention was turned to bringing home the constitution. None of the premiers could agree on what reforms would be entrenched in the new Charter, so Trudeau went ahead and wrote up the constitution himself, to the delight of hundreds of lawyers across the country, who expanded their offices and hired extra staff, in anticipation of the flood of court challenges to the new, vague Charter of Rights.

Native leaders were at first fairly optimistic about their aboriginal rights being recognized in the Charter, but after reading the fine print they realized they would have no say should any future government choose to remove the few rights they had won. Quebec refused to sign the new constitution, because it did not allow Quebec to remain a "distinct society" or give them the power of veto under the Charter.

The country came together briefly to mourn Marathon of Hope runner, Terry Fox, who died of cancer June 28, 1981, after abandoning his run for cancer research at Thunder Bay.

A few British MPs who dragged themselves out of the House of Commons bar and found their way to the Chamber voted to send the constitution back to Canada. Just in time for the Queen to stick her "Lizzie II" on the new document in Ottawa. Pierre Trudeau's claim that he had strengthened the rights of English-speaking Canadians in Quebec was drowned out by the noise of fleets of moving trucks leaving Hull, Quebec, on the way to Ontario. Politically, Pierre disappeared in an Ottawa snowstorm, leaving behind two million man-years of work for constitutional lawyers.

Joe Clark, the walking pincushion, with an impressive collection of Liberal and Tory knives in his back, finally gave in to the humiliation and resigned as leader, after being beaten by Brian Mulroney, who

finally clawed his way to the top (or bottom, depending on which way you look at it). Mulroney was to have *his* day in the sun (and latterly, most of them in the shade), but that's a whole other story. . . .

From the time the Norsemen departed these shores, until Trudeau left us high and dry, we boat people have all had a role in how this country has turned out. In some places, we've turned pleasant real estate into septic tanks. In others, we've preserved *some* of the wilderness, we've repelled American invasions, done our part in liberating Europe (twice), built a pretty nifty railroad (then shut it down) and come up with a constitution of our very own (at least Trudeau did). All of this on land that doesn't *technically* belong to us.

It would be easy to gaze out the window at our handiwork (during commercial breaks) and reflect on the past. But what we should be doing is throwing up barricades and grabbing pitchforks, otherwise the land our ancestors cleared with their bare hands will be turned into trendy golf courses, our marshland will be suffocating under more mini malls, our few remaining forests will end up as toothpicks, and what's left will be loaded onto a truck and moved south.

Then there won't be any neighbourhood.

Still, despite a rather chequered past and an uncertain future, Canada remains unquestionably the best country in the world, and one of the few places where we have the freedom to write a book like *There Goes The Neighbourhood*. A book which in many countries . . . hang on, there's a knock at the . . .